CCSS | **Genre** | Expository Text

Essential Question
What are the positive and negative effects of new technology?

What About
ROBOTS?

BY YVONNE MORRIN

We use technology every day. We have machines to transport us and to wash our clothes. Other machines keep our food fresh, help us communicate, and entertain us. Our lives would be very different if we didn't have technology!

Technology is advancing all the time. Some people are excited about these changes. Others are worried about them. Can you think of some of the positive effects of new technology? What about some possible negative effects? What is your reasoning?

One area of technology that is advancing rapidly is **robotics**. There are millions of robots in the world. Most do jobs that are considered too dangerous or too boring for humans. Many people think robots are useful to society. Others believe that people might become too dependent on robots or that robots might take their jobs. Imagine being replaced by a robot!

Before forming an opinion about robotics, it is important to look at the facts. Then you can weigh the advantages and the disadvantages. This helps you to make thoughtful conclusions. It also allows you to cite evidence that backs up your reasoning and supports your opinion.

Technology affects many areas of our lives.

CHAPTER 1

What Is a Robot?

The word *robot* comes from the Czech word *robota*, which means "forced labor."

Robots come in many shapes and sizes.

There are many definitions of what a robot is. One definition is that a robot is a machine that operates automatically in place of a human to complete a task. This definition would fit a washing machine.

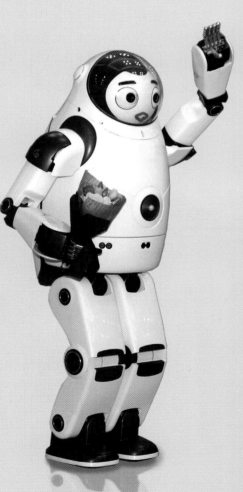

A washing machine carries out the task of washing clothes. It takes the place of a human washing the clothes by hand. Yet most people would not consider a washing machine to be a robot.

A better definition is that a robot is a machine that uses information from its surroundings to make decisions about what to do. The machine interacts with its environment to achieve a goal.

This kind of robot acts as if it has intelligence. It has equipment, such as cameras or microphones, to take in information. A computer responds to the information and makes decisions. Then the mechanical parts of the robot pick up and move objects to complete a task.

Robots Through History

Between 1700 and 1900, a number of inventors created life-sized mechanical people and animals. These inventions had moving parts and were called **automatons**. Some automatons could play musical instruments and draw pictures. However, automatons do not process information about their environments. As a result, they are not considered true robots.

The first machine that was able to make decisions was built in 1911. It played chess against humans. It used electrical **sensors** to figure out where the chess pieces were on the board. Then it moved a mechanical arm to take its turn.

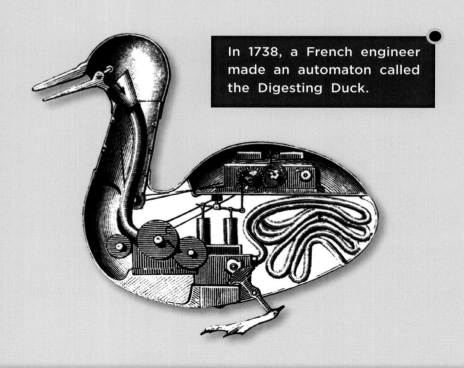

In 1738, a French engineer made an automaton called the Digesting Duck.

FICTIONAL ROBOTS

Long before real robots were invented, science fiction stories set in the future included robots. Some of the movies of the 1920s and 1930s showed robots plotting to take over Earth! Later, when robots came to television in the 1950s and 1960s, they were often shown as helpful companions.

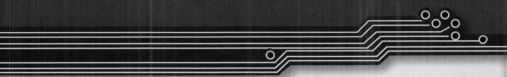

Then, in the mid-twentieth century, computer technology developed to the point where machines could be controlled by **artificial** brains. These were the first true robots.

The first machine that was able to move freely and interact with its environment was made in the 1940s. It rolled around on three wheels. This machine could make decisions about how to avoid objects. It moved so slowly that it was called Elsie the Tortoise.

CHAPTER 2

Robots at Work

These robots are assembling cars on a production line.

The first robot designed to work in a factory had a heavy lifting arm. Its movements were controlled by **electronics**. It could be programmed to perform different actions. In 1961, the robot was used in a factory that built cars. It lifted metal parts that were too hot for humans to handle.

Robots began to be used in American factories in the 1960s and 1970s. Although robots are expensive, they can save a company money over time. That's because they:

- can often do jobs faster and more accurately than a human can;

- don't get tired and make mistakes;

- don't get bored of doing the same task over and over again.

These robots changed factory work. However, some people worried that robots would take people's jobs. They also worried about safety. In 1988, some incorrectly programmed robots began smashing windows and painting each other!

Although industrial robots first appeared in the United States, most were **manufactured** in Japan and Europe by the 1980s. Japan has an aging population. People were concerned that there would not be enough young workers. They thought robots would be needed in the future.

INDUSTRIAL ROBOT LOCATIONS

Asia leads the world in robot use.

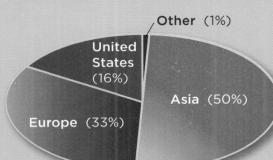

Other (1%)

United States (16%)

Asia (50%)

Europe (33%)

VIEWPOINTS
ROBOTS IN THE WORKPLACE

"I think having robots at work is a good idea. They can do all the dangerous jobs."

"If we start using robots instead of humans at work, will I lose my job and be replaced by a machine?"

What do you think? Is it a good idea to have robots in the workplace?

Too Dangerous for Humans!

Robots are very useful when it comes to dangerous jobs. They can be used to clean up chemical spills and **toxic** waste in nuclear plants. Robots can even **defuse** bombs.

Robots can also be used when there is a disaster, such as an earthquake. This can be a dangerous situation. There may be fires or gas leaks, or damaged walls could collapse. The rescuers who search for survivors put their own lives at risk. That's why robotic scouts were developed. These robots perform searches and make rescuing survivors safer.

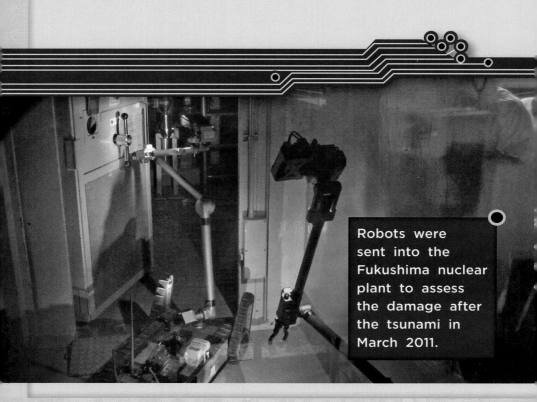

Robots were sent into the Fukushima nuclear plant to assess the damage after the tsunami in March 2011.

Robotic scouts can access dangerous areas while carrying cameras and gas detectors, which send important information back to the rescuers. These data help the rescuers with their analysis of the situation. Robots can carry food, medicine, air tanks, and two-way radios to trapped survivors. Some robots are even designed to drag survivors out of wreckage.

Space is another risky environment for humans. Engineers have developed a robotic astronaut. This robot can roll over the surface of planets exploring the **terrain** and then pick up samples with its hands. Unlike a human, the robot doesn't need to breathe, eat, or keep warm.

This robotic astronaut is connected to a vehicle called a rover.

CHAPTER 3

New Uses for Robots

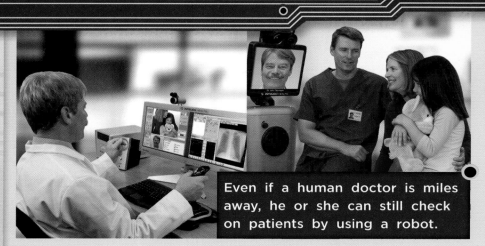

Even if a human doctor is miles away, he or she can still check on patients by using a robot.

As scientists develop more advanced technology, they find new uses for robots.

Robots in Hospitals

Many hospitals now use robots to help care for patients. Robots can deliver food or dispense medicine. Using robots reduces the risk of disease being spread to staff members. It also frees up nurses to perform other jobs.

However, there are drawbacks to using robots for patient care. Some people are frightened of them. Others don't trust them not to make errors. Many patients feel more comfortable interacting with another human rather than with a machine.

SURGICAL ROBOT OPERATIONS

This graph shows that the number of operations performed by one brand of surgical robot increased every year between 2005 and 2010. More growth is predicted.

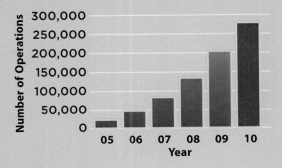

Surgical robots are becoming more popular. Human surgeons control these robots. The robots are used to perform complex operations. Robots have been used for heart operations, brain surgery, and kidney transplants.

A surgical robot can be more precise than a human surgeon. Without big hands and fingers, the robot can make smaller cuts in patients. As a result, the cuts heal faster.

VIEWPOINTS
ROBOTIC NURSING ASSISTANTS

Japan has a large elderly population. Some people like the idea of robotic nursing assistants, but others don't.

"I don't like having a robot deliver my pills. I don't trust the robot to get it right. I'm lonely, and I want to talk to a real person."

"It's good that the robots deliver my meals. It means nurses can spend more time with the people who need attention."

What do you think? Would you like a robot as your nurse?

"Robots might be able to solve almost all of our environmental problems. We should spend more money on developing new robots to clean up the environment."

"Until we can produce robots in a more environmentally friendly way, we shouldn't produce more. Spend money on preventing environmental problems first."

What do you think? Are robots good or bad for the environment?

Friend of the Environment?

Many people are **wary** of society's increasing use of robots. They feel that robots are environmentally unfriendly. They say that robots are made out of materials that need to be mined, and mining can damage the environment.

People also argue that factories that make robots use up **resources**, such as fuel and water. Throwing away outdated technology from robots can also harm the environment.

Computers contain poisonous chemicals. If these chemicals are not disposed of carefully, they can harm the environment.

This robot floats on the surface of the ocean and cleans up oil that is harmful to marine life.

However, the counterpoint is that robots can be very helpful to the environment. Engineers are inventing robots that can be used to check the health of the environment and clean up **pollutants**. Some robots even use eco-friendly solar panels to collect energy from the sun.

The future might be full of robots helping to improve the environment. Already people have designed robots that can sort plastic for recycling, plant trees, and filter pollution out of the air.

Learning from Animals

What is intelligence? Some people think intelligence means being good at analyzing data or solving puzzles. Others believe intelligence means being able to make decisions in response to the environment.

Animals are very good at surviving in their environments. Many engineers are now turning to animals for ideas for robots.

The rat-robot has touch sensors in its whiskers, cameras in its eye sockets, and microphones in its ears. The inventor says, "We want to make robots that are able to look after themselves." The rat-robot can be used in dark, smoke-filled rooms, or even underground.

The rat-robot is small enough to fit into places humans can't easily go.

There are robots that have many legs so that they can walk over rough ground the way a spider does. Others can hover like a hummingbird.

Conclusion

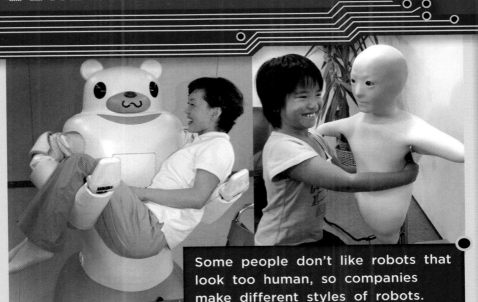

Some people don't like robots that look too human, so companies make different styles of robots.

In the future, inventors will come up with new uses for robots. Robots will more often care for the sick, solve environmental problems, help in disasters, and make workplaces safer. As a result, many people will develop positive opinions about the work robots do.

However, there will still be people who don't approve of robots. They might fear that people will start to rely on robots too much or lose important skills. Others might feel uncomfortable around robots and prefer another person to a machine.

When companies design new robots, they will have to consider all of these opinions in order to make robots that people will be willing to use.

Respond to Reading

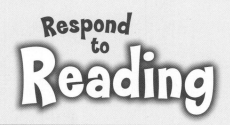

Summarize

Use details from the text to summarize the positive and negative effects of robots. Your graphic organizer may help you.

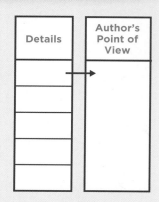

Text Evidence

1. What features of *What About Robots?* tell you it is an expository text? **GENRE**

2. What point of view does the author reveal in Chapter 3 of *What About Robots?* What details from the text support this? **AUTHOR'S POINT OF VIEW**

3. The Greek prefix *auto-* means "self" or "same." Using this and context clues, figure out the meaning of *automatically* on page 4. Then find another word in the text that has this prefix and explain its meaning. **GREEK AND LATIN PREFIXES**

4. Write about the author's position on robots. Do you think the author is pro-robot or anti-robot? Use details from the text in your answer. **WRITE ABOUT READING**

Compare Texts
Read an argument against using robots.

No
Substitute

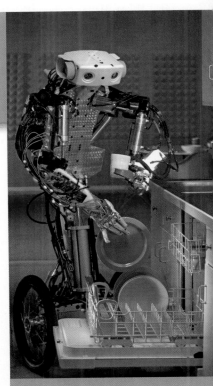

This robot was designed to help around the house.

Some people say that in the future, every home will have a robot. Many people think this will be a wonderful change. They say it will free up time for busy people and make their lives better. In this essay, I hope to persuade you that a robot in every home would be a terrible thing.

People who rely on a machine to do household chores will become lazy. Children who don't have to help at home might never learn the value of hard work. By not taking responsibility for messes they make, humans might stop taking responsibility for their actions.

Several companies in Japan and Korea have developed child-care robots. But parents or other human caregivers have a responsibility to raise children. They must teach their children how to behave. This is not something a robot can do because robots aren't capable of feeling emotions.

Robots can't interact with children the way people do. They can't show **compassion**, sympathy, or love. Children raised by a robot might not fully develop their emotions.

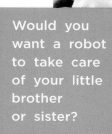

Would you want a robot to take care of your little brother or sister?

20

There are safety issues too. Robots can only do what they are programmed to do. This means that a robot could do something dangerous if something unexpected happened. In an emergency, the robot might not respond at all if it were not programmed to deal with the problem.

What if something went wrong while a robot was in charge? Would it be the fault of the robot, the robot's programmer, the robot's user, or the robot's owner?

Finally, what would happen to the human workers the robots replaced? Many people work as house cleaners, babysitters, or nurse companions. If robots took over this work, many people would lose their jobs.

For all of these reasons, it is clear that a robot in every home is not a good idea.

Make Connections

What does *No Substitute* identify as the negative effects of using robots? ESSENTIAL QUESTION

After reading both texts, what is your point of view about robots? TEXT TO TEXT

Glossary

artificial *(ahr-tuh-FISH-uhl)* not natural; made by humans *(page 7)*

automatons *(aw-TOM-uh-tonz)* machines that follow a set of instructions; some look like humans or animals *(page 6)*

compassion *(kuhm-PASH-uhn)* a deep feeling of sympathy for someone else and a strong desire to help *(page 20)*

defuse *(dee-FYEWZ)* remove the fuse from a bomb so that it can't explode *(page 10)*

electronics *(i-lek-TRON-iks)* electrical circuits, devices, and equipment *(page 8)*

manufactured *(man-yuh-FAK-chuhrd)* made or produced *(page 9)*

pollutants *(puh-LEW-tuhnts)* things that are harmful to the environment *(page 15)*

resources *(REE-sawrs-iz)* things that are useful to humans; for example, water, fuel, and food *(page 14)*

robotics *(roh-BOT-iks)* the branch of technology that deals with how robots are designed, built, and used *(page 3)*

sensors *(SEN-suhrz)* devices that can detect things, such as movement or light *(page 6)*

terrain *(tuh-RAYN)* the surface of the land *(page 11)*

toxic *(TOK-sik)* poisonous *(page 10)*

wary *(WAYR-ee)* cautious *(page 14)*

Index

Focus on Science

Purpose To explore what robots can and cannot do

Procedure

Step 1 Use the Internet to research current developments in robotics and learn more about what robots can and cannot do.

Step 2 Make a two-column chart labeled "Can" and "Cannot." As you learn more about robots, record what they can and cannot do on your chart.

Step 3 Now make a chart for humans and record some of the things that humans can and cannot do.

Step 4 After conducting your research, what is your opinion about robots versus humans? Use information from your charts to create a poster, a slide presentation, or a skit that compares robots with humans. Make sure you clearly show your point of view.

Conclusion Do you think the use of robots will become more common, less common, or stay about the same as it is now? Why?